DESTINATION SPACE

# THE SPACE SHUTTLE MISSIONS

by Patti Richards

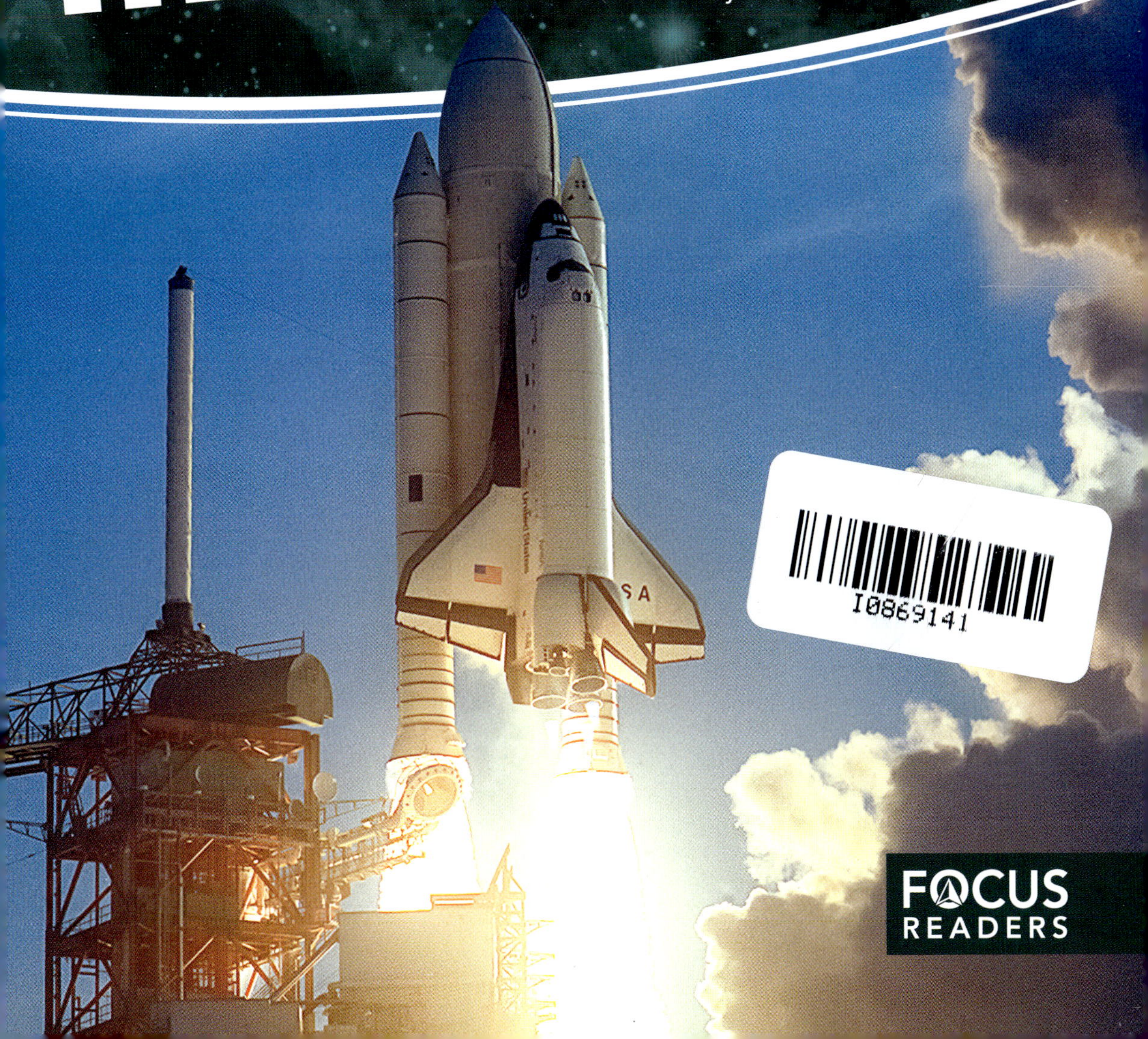



FOCUS READERS

FOCUS READERS

www.focusreaders.com



Focus Readers is distributed by North Star Editions:
sales@northstareditions.com | 888-417-0195

Produced for Focus Readers by Red Line Editorial.

Content Consultant: James Flaten, Associate Director of NASA's MN Space Grant Consortium and Contract Associate Professor, Aerospace Engineering and Mechanics Department, University of Minnesota–Twin Cities

Photographs ©: MSFC/NASA, cover, 1, 10–11, 40–41, 43; JSC/NASA, 4–5, 13, 20–21, 23, 27, 28–29, 31, 33, 34–35; NACA/NASA Langely Research Center/LRC/NASA, 7; Red Line Editorial, 9; ARC/NASA, 14–15; MightyRabittCrew/Shutterstock Images, 17; CXC/JPL/NASA, 19; Bruce Weaver/AP Images, 25; NASA, 37; KSC/NASA, 39; Bill Ingalls/HQ/NASA, 44

**ISBN**
978-1-63517-498-4 (hardcover)
978-1-63517-570-7 (paperback)
978-1-63517-714-5 (ebook pdf)
978-1-63517-642-1 (hosted ebook)

**Library of Congress Control Number: 2017948060**

Printed in the United States of America
Mankato, MN
November, 2017

## ABOUT THE AUTHOR

Patti Richards is a writer, editor, and former teacher. She is the author of two books (*Snow Angels* and *All About Social Networking*) and several short stories featured in Amazon Rapids, *Highlights Magazine*, and *Boys' Quest*. Patti and her family live in southeast Michigan.

# TABLE OF CONTENTS

CHAPTER 1

# TO SPACE AND BACK

By the early 1970s, astronauts had landed on the moon and studied its surface. Many people thought space exploration would soon end. But scientists were just beginning to explore space. In 1972, US President Richard Nixon signed a bill that gave $5.5 million to the National Aeronautics and Space Administration (NASA). This organization had been created in 1958 to control the United States' activity in space.

**Astronauts aboard a space shuttle took this photo of Earth in 1990.**

NASA had sent astronauts to the moon as part of the Apollo missions. Now, it had a new project. NASA would use the money to design space shuttles. These reusable vehicles would take people into outer space and back again. Scientists hoped the shuttles would make space travel easier, safer, and less expensive than ever before.

Designing a spacecraft that could be used multiple times was challenging. A space shuttle needed a way to launch, carry fuel, and return to Earth. But NASA scientists were already hard at work. Between 1959 and 1968, they designed and built several prototypes. Prototypes are early versions of inventions that are created to test an idea. NASA used the prototypes to try out designs for space shuttles. One was a rocket-powered airplane known as the X-15. X-15s made 199 test flights. During these flights,

A NASA scientist tests a model of the X-15 by hanging it underneath a model of a bomber.

NASA learned about **hypersonic** flight. The X-15's success helped NASA prepare to create a space shuttle.

NASA's space shuttle program officially began in 1972. The shuttle design had three main parts.

Each shuttle would have an orbiter, an external fuel tank, and rocket boosters. The orbiter looked like an airplane. Astronauts would live in this part of the shuttle during their trips to space. The external fuel tank would carry liquid fuel for the shuttle to use during its journey. Each shuttle also used two rocket boosters. These solid-fuel rockets would attach to either side of the shuttle's huge fuel tank. The boosters would help launch the shuttle into space.

However, designing a shuttle was only the beginning. NASA needed to test each part to make sure it worked. By 1976, NASA was ready to test the shuttle's orbiter. NASA scientists needed to make sure it could bring astronauts safely back to Earth. So, they created the Approach and Landing Test (ALT) program. This program made sure the orbiter could glide and land properly.

# SPACE SHUTTLE PARTS

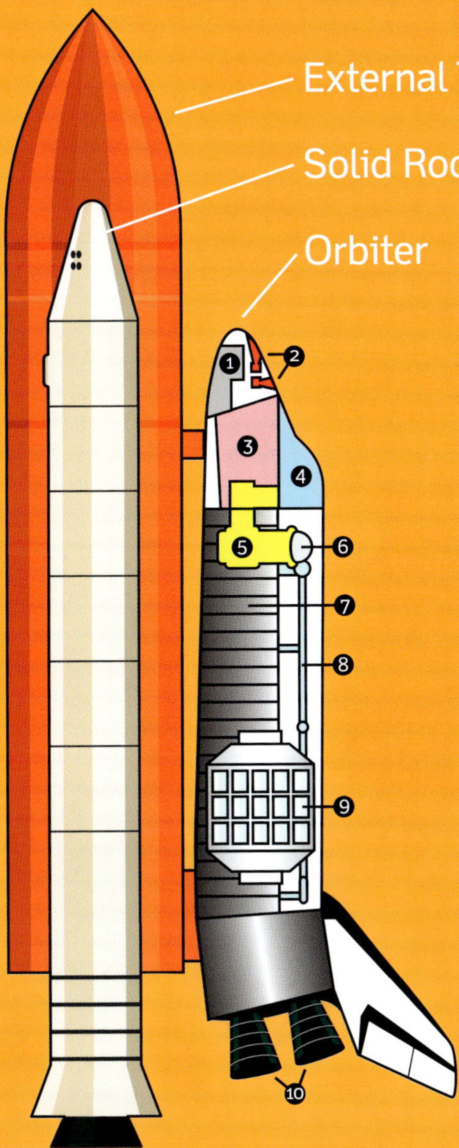


1. Nose landing gear
2. Steering thrusters
3. Mid-deck
4. Flight deck
5. Airlock
6. Docking port
7. Cargo bay
8. Robotic arm
9. Cargo module
10. Main rocket engines

Enterprise
United States
NASA

CHAPTER 2

# THE *ENTERPRISE* ORBITER

The *Enterprise* orbiter was completed in September 1976. The orbiter was not designed to go to space. Instead, it was used for the ALT program. For nine months, two crews of astronauts performed many tests using the *Enterprise* orbiter. Fred Haise and Gordon Fullerton were one crew. Joe Engle and Dick Truly were the other.

**The *Enterprise* orbiter went through many tests at the Marshall Space Flight Center in Alabama.**

First, crew members did ground tests. These tests made sure the orbiter's systems worked properly. For some of these tests, the *Enterprise* rode on the back of a 747 carrier airplane. Pilots checked the steering, braking, handling, and control of the carrier with the shuttle attached. They made sure the orbiter's systems worked as planned.

After these tests, the crews were ready to try glide flights. For this phase of testing, the *Enterprise* separated from the carrier aircraft while in the air. Crew members took turns steering the orbiter as it glided. They also practiced landing.

## THINK ABOUT IT

**Why do you think NASA had two different crews test the *Enterprise* orbiter?**

The *Enterprise* orbiter (top) separates from the NASA 747 carrier.

During the final phase of the ALT program, the orbiter went through vertical ground vibration tests. For these tests, engineers connected an external tank and solid rocket boosters to the orbiter. These tests helped them prepare to launch an orbiter. Shuttle testing with the *Enterprise* ended in March 1979. It was now time to try launching a shuttle into space.

United States
USA

CHAPTER 3

# FROM TRAILBLAZING TO TRAGEDY

Two years after the last test of the *Enterprise*, NASA built the first complete space shuttle. Its orbiter was named *Columbia*. *Columbia*'s first mission took place in April 1981. The two rocket boosters and the orbiter's engines helped create thrust. This pushing force propelled the shuttle into space. Two minutes after launch, the boosters dropped off the shuttle. They landed in the ocean. Boats retrieved them so they could be used again.

***Columbia* was the first space shuttle to launch into space and return to Earth.**

After the shuttle used nearly all the fuel in its external tank, the tank dropped off the shuttle as well. Unlike the boosters, the tank burned up in Earth's atmosphere. Only the orbiter was left. During this first mission, *Columbia* **orbited** Earth a total of 36 times. Then the orbiter returned to Earth and landed like an airplane.

In November 1983, *Columbia* was launched carrying a reusable science laboratory known as Spacelab. Carried inside the orbiter's cargo bay, Spacelab was made up of two sections. One section was a **pressurized** laboratory. It held many kinds of scientific equipment. Astronauts used the equipment to perform experiments while the shuttle orbited Earth. Spacelab's other section was a carrier. This section held telescopes, antennas, and sensors. These instruments collected information about space.

# LAUNCHING THE SPACE SHUTTLE

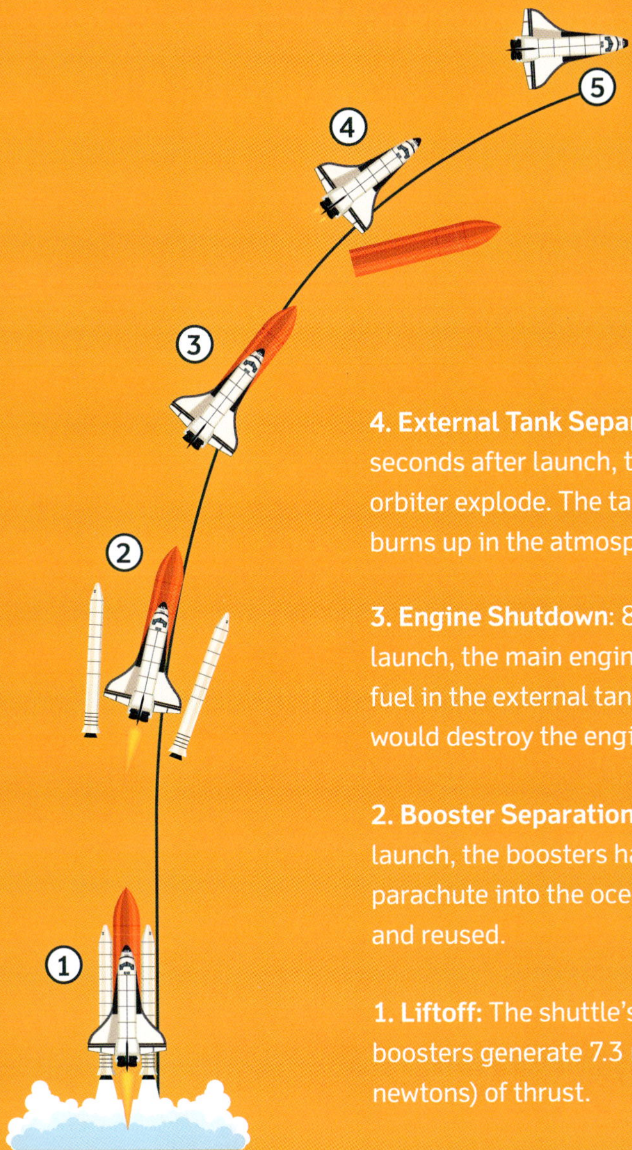


**5. Orbit**: Small rockets attached to the orbiter fire, putting the shuttle into stable orbit. At this time, the shuttle is 230 miles (370 km) above Earth and traveling at 17,500 miles per hour (28,164 km/h).

**4. External Tank Separation**: 8 minutes and 40 seconds after launch, the bolts holding the tank to the orbiter explode. The tank falls back toward Earth and burns up in the atmosphere.

**3. Engine Shutdown**: 8 minutes and 24 seconds after launch, the main engines shut down just before the fuel in the external tank runs out. Burning the tank dry would destroy the engines.

**2. Booster Separation**: 2 minutes and 7 seconds after launch, the boosters have used up their fuel. They parachute into the ocean, where they will be recovered and reused.

**1. Liftoff:** The shuttle's main engines and rocket boosters generate 7.3 million pounds (32 million newtons) of thrust.

*Columbia* was the first shuttle to carry Spacelab. But Spacelab would eventually fly at least once on every shuttle in the space shuttle program.

One of *Columbia*'s greatest accomplishments happened in July 1999. *Columbia* and its crew **deployed** the Chandra X-Ray Observatory. This telescope detects X-rays that are given off by **deep space** objects.

Unfortunately, *Columbia*'s groundbreaking career was cut short. On February 1, 2003, the orbiter was supposed to land in Florida. However, as the shuttle came back into Earth's atmosphere, the orbiter broke apart. All seven crew members were killed. Their names were Rick Husband, Michael Anderson, Ilan Ramon, Kalpana Chawla, David Brown, William McCool, and Laurel Clark.

NASA was determined to find out what caused the accident. A team of investigators discovered

The Chandra X-Ray Observatory orbits above Earth's atmosphere.

that a piece of foam insulation had come loose from the shuttle's fuel tank. Not long after the shuttle launched, the insulation had broken off and damaged the inside of the shuttle's left wing. As the damaged orbiter began to land, hot gases leaked in and destroyed the inside of the wing. This caused the shuttle to break apart.

Challenger
NASA
United States

## CHAPTER 4

# THE *CHALLENGER* DISASTER

The second complete shuttle, called *Challenger*, used a new, lighter design for its orbiter. NASA needed to make sure it could withstand the harsh environment of space. After a year of testing, NASA was satisfied. *Challenger* was ready to launch. The shuttle's first mission began in April 1983. The mission included the shuttle program's first **space walk**. Crew members also deployed a **satellite** and conducted research.

***Challenger* made a total of 10 trips into space.**

In June 1983, Sally Ride was part of the crew for *Challenger*'s second mission. She became the first female American astronaut to go to space. Kathryn Sullivan joined Ride on a mission in October 1984. This made *Challenger* the first shuttle to carry two female astronauts. During the mission, Sullivan became the first American woman to go on a space walk.

The shuttle's tenth mission began in January 1986. Its crew included Christa McAuliffe. She was a social studies teacher from New Hampshire. She was chosen as part of the Teacher in Space program. McAuliffe would become the first ordinary citizen to travel on a space shuttle. During the mission, she planned to use a live video feed. She would teach lessons about space to children around the United States. Other crew members were Gregory Jarvis, Judith Resnik,

In 1984, *Challenger*'s crew included Ride (front row, center left) and Sullivan (front row, center right).

Francis Scobee, Ronald McNair, Michael Smith, and Ellison Onizuka.

*Challenger* was originally scheduled to lift off on January 22. But weather and other problems kept the shuttle on the ground for six days. January 28 was an unusually cold morning at the Kennedy Space Center in Cape Canaveral, Florida.

Space shuttle engineers were concerned that some parts of the shuttle would not work in the cold weather. For example, they thought the shuttle's O-rings might fail. These rubber rings sealed the joints of the rocket boosters. But NASA decided to go ahead with the mission.

People all over the United States watched on TV as *Challenger* got ready to launch. The shuttle lifted off at 11:39 a.m. Only 73 seconds later, the spacecraft broke apart and fell into the ocean in a cloud of fire and smoke. All seven astronauts died in the crash. Millions of shocked viewers watched the disaster happen.

## THINK ABOUT IT

**Why do you think NASA decided to launch *Challenger* despite the cold weather?**

*Challenger* exploded shortly after liftoff from the Kennedy Space Center.

President Ronald Reagan put together a task force to find out what went wrong. This group found that the shuttle's O-rings had failed. As a result, flames from the rocket booster damaged the fuel tank. All space shuttle flights were stopped until NASA could solve the problems that caused the accident.

# SALLY RIDE

Sally Ride was born in Los Angeles, California, in 1951. She loved to play sports, especially tennis. She competed in tournaments throughout the United States. After high school, Ride studied English and physics at Stanford University. She graduated in 1973 and continued to study physics. After receiving her doctorate in physics in 1978, she applied to NASA's astronaut training program. Ride became part of the first class that included women. She trained for five years. Then she was chosen to be part of *Challenger*'s crew.

During her first mission in 1983, Ride spent seven days in space. Her second mission in 1984 lasted eight days. During both trips, Ride helped conduct research. She had planned to go to space a third time. But when the *Challenger* shuttle exploded, Ride joined the group that investigated the accident. Afterward, she worked for NASA

Sally Ride made two journeys to space aboard the *Challenger* space shuttle.

as an administrator. In this role, she helped plan many missions.

Ride left NASA in 1989 to become a professor. She taught physics at the University of California San Diego. She also directed the school's California Space Institute. In 2001, Ride founded a company called Sally Ride Science. The company was designed to help women get jobs related to science and math. Ride died of cancer in 2012. Throughout her life, she worked to help more people study science.

Discovery

## CHAPTER 5

# SATELLITES, SPACECRAFT, AND *DISCOVERY*

NASA's third shuttle orbiter was called *Discovery*. During its first mission in August 1984, it launched three communications satellites. These satellites joined the satellite deployed during the first *Challenger* mission. Together, they formed part of the Tracking and Data Relay System (TDRS) constellation. The TDRS is a group of nine satellites that constantly send and receive information as they orbit Earth.

**This photo of *Discovery* was taken by astronauts on the International Space Station.**

These satellites help with communication during other NASA projects.

In April 1990, *Discovery* deployed the Hubble Space Telescope. Hubble is a large orbiting telescope. It takes photographs and gathers information about planets, stars, galaxies, and other objects in space. *Discovery* went on two more missions to repair and upgrade the telescope.

During the 1990s, *Discovery* made several flights carrying science labs and instruments. It also deployed spacecraft. In 1990, *Discovery* carried the *Ulysses* spacecraft. This spacecraft helped study the sun. Another spacecraft was deployed in 1991 to analyze Earth's upper atmosphere. *Discovery* also visited the Russian space station Mir. Its first visit was in 1995. It returned again in 1999.

Between 1986 and 1996, Mir was launched in pieces that were joined together in space.

*Discovery* helped construct the International Space Station (ISS) as well. The ISS is a giant spacecraft that orbits Earth. Many countries worked together to build it. Because of its massive size, the ISS had to be sent to space in pieces.

Space shuttles brought one piece, or module, at a time. Then astronauts connected the modules together in space.

*Discovery* **docked** at the ISS for the first time in 1999. The shuttle returned to the ISS 12 more times, including its final flight in February 2011. During this last mission, *Discovery* attached a new module to the ISS. Two days after launching, *Discovery* docked at the ISS. *Discovery*'s crew met with the space station's six residents. This was the first time spacecraft from Russia, Japan, Europe, and the United States were all at the ISS at the same time. For the next week, *Discovery*'s crew helped get the new module ready to use. Then the shuttle headed back to Earth for the last time.

During its long career, the *Discovery* shuttle flew 39 missions. It spent a total of 365 days in space. That is more than any other orbiter.

Frederick Gregory (left) undergoes training in the Shuttle Mission Simulator in 1991.

*Discovery* also carried more astronauts than any other shuttle. These astronauts set several records. For instance, Frederick Gregory became the first African-American commander to fly a space shuttle in 1989. *Discovery* also had the first female space shuttle pilot. Eileen Collins flew the shuttle in 1995 during its mission to Mir.

USA

CHAPTER 6

# ATLANTIS AND SPACE EXPLORATION

NASA began building a fourth space shuttle in 1980. Known as *Atlantis*, the shuttle launched for the first time in October 1985. It carried a secret **payload** for the US Department of Defense.

During later missions, the *Atlantis* shuttle deployed two space probes. The first, known as *Magellan*, was released in May 1989 and traveled to Venus. After entering orbit in August 1990, *Magellan* used radar to map the planet's surface.

***Atlantis* releases the *Magellan* probe from its cargo bay.**

*Magellan* sent back images of channels and winds on Venus. NASA lost contact with the probe in 1994. But by that time, *Magellan* had mapped 98 percent of the planet's surface. This was much more than NASA's original goal of 70 percent.

*Atlantis* deployed the *Galileo* probe in October 1989. This probe traveled all the way to Jupiter. It arrived in December 1995. *Galileo* orbited Jupiter for two years, collecting information about the planet's atmosphere and weather. Between 1997 and 2001, the probe also collected data about Jupiter's moons.

In 1995, *Atlantis* became the first space shuttle to dock with Mir. *Atlantis* returned to Mir six times. These missions helped NASA learn more about life in space and prepare to build the ISS. Later on, *Atlantis* carried several modules of the ISS into orbit.

In 1995, *Atlantis* and Mir formed what was the largest spacecraft in orbit at that time.

During most of the shuttle's missions, crew members conducted science experiments. They did research while the shuttle was in orbit. Crew members studied how spending time in space affects plants and people's bodies.

# THE GLASS COCKPIT

In 2000, engineers made several improvements to the *Atlantis* shuttle. One of the most important changes was the new Multifunction Electronic Display System (MEDS). This system used glass screens to replace many old flight instruments. For this reason, it was called the glass cockpit.

NASA engineers began working to develop the MEDS in the 1970s. They used technology that had been created for commercial airplanes. At the time, most airplanes had more than 100 instruments in their cockpits. Keeping track of so much information could be overwhelming for pilots. So, engineers created a computerized system that tracked information about the plane. The system presented the key information on a screen. Pilots could easily find the information they needed. NASA modified this technology to create the MEDS. The system's 11 screens

The MEDS stretched from one side of the shuttle's cockpit to the other.

displayed information about the shuttle. Pilots could easily find and read key details such as the shuttle's altitude or speed.

*Atlantis* was the first space shuttle to use this new technology. The MEDS was much lighter than the shuttle's old instruments. It also took less power to run. Plus, liquid crystal display (LCD) screens were easy to read from many angles. And they did not create glare in the sun's light. This helped pilots avoid accidents or errors.

Endeavour
CUT HERE FOR EMERGENCY RESCUE
NASA

## CHAPTER 7

# THE LAST SHUTTLE

NASA began building the last space shuttle, *Endeavour*, in 1987. This was the year after *Challenger* exploded. *Endeavour* was intended to replace it.

*Endeavour*'s first mission took place in May 1992. During the mission, crew members worked to capture a communications satellite that needed repairs. This was a difficult task. The satellite was not designed to dock with the space shuttle.

**Seven astronauts made up *Endeavour*'s first crew.**

The crew and **mission control** worked hard to find a way to grab onto the satellite to fix it. It took the crew three tries to capture the satellite. After attaching a new motor to the satellite, they sent it back into orbit.

During this mission, *Endeavour*'s crew performed the first three-person space walk. It was also the first time astronauts made four separate space walks during a single space shuttle mission. One walk lasted more than eight hours, making it the longest space walk yet.

*Endeavour* flew a total of 25 missions, including 12 missions to help build the ISS.

## THINK ABOUT IT

**What are some challenges astronauts might face during a space walk?**

The three astronauts grabbed the Intelsat VI satellite and pulled it into the shuttle's cargo bay.

Astronauts conducted many experiments during the shuttle's flights. They studied how living in space affects the human body.

*Endeavour*'s last mission was in May 2011. The space shuttle program was nearing an end as well.

*Atlantis* blasted off for its last mission on July 8, 2011.

Despite NASA's plans, space travel was still expensive. The shuttles had needed constant repairs and upgrades. NASA's budget could not continue to support the program. In 2004, President George W. Bush had announced that NASA would phase out the space shuttle program. *Discovery*, *Atlantis*, and *Endeavour* would continue to help complete the ISS. Then shuttle flights would end. Money that had been used for the shuttles would fund new projects.

*Atlantis* made the final flight of the space shuttle program. It took a four-person crew to the ISS in July 2011. The crew delivered 9,400 pounds (4,264 kg) of spare parts, equipment, supplies, and food. These supplies were enough to keep the ISS running for a year. Then *Atlantis* began the journey back to Earth.

On July 21, *Atlantis* touched down on the runway at the Kennedy Space Center. The space shuttle program was officially over. The *Atlantis* orbiter would stay at the Kennedy Space Center. *Discovery*, *Endeavour*, and *Enterprise* were sent to museums around the United States. At each location, visitors could glimpse the amazing engineering that brought people to and from space for more than 30 years.

FOCUS ON

# THE SPACE SHUTTLE MISSIONS

*Write your answers on a separate piece of paper.*

**1.** Write a paragraph describing the three parts of the space shuttle and explaining how each part was used.

**2.** Do you think the space shuttle program lived up to the hope of making space travel easier, safer, and less expensive? Why or why not?

**3.** Which space shuttle flew the most missions?

- **A.** *Columbia*
- **B.** *Discovery*
- **C.** *Endeavour*

**4.** Why did NASA investigate what caused the *Columbia* shuttle to fall apart?

- **A.** so NASA could use the pieces to build another shuttle
- **B.** so NASA could complete its mission's goal
- **C.** so NASA could prevent a similar problem in other shuttles

*Answer key on page 48.*

# GLOSSARY

**deep space**
Far outside Earth's atmosphere, especially beyond the moon.

**deployed**
Carried something into orbit and then released it into space.

**docked**
Joined together while in space.

**hypersonic**
At least five times as fast as the speed of sound.

**mission control**
The team of engineers and experts running a mission from the ground.

**orbited**
Repeatedly followed a curved path around another object because of gravity.

**payload**
An object carried to space by a rocket or other vehicle.

**pressurized**
When part of an airplane or spacecraft is sealed off so that the air pressure in that part can be kept at safe levels for people inside it.

**satellite**
An object or vehicle that orbits a planet or moon, often to collect information.

**space walk**
When an astronaut goes outside a spacecraft and moves around in space.

# TO LEARN MORE

## BOOKS


Etingoff, Kim. *The Space Shuttle Program*. Vestal, NY: Village Earth Press, 2014.

Holden, Henry M. *Space Shuttle Disaster: The Tragic Mission of the Challenger*. Berkeley Heights, NJ: Enslow Publishers, 2013.

Langley, Andrew. *Sally Ride and the Shuttle Missions*. Chicago: Heinemann Raintree, 2016.


## NOTE TO EDUCATORS

Visit **www.focusreaders.com** to find lesson plans, activities, links, and other resources related to this title.

# INDEX



**Answer Key: 1.** Answers will vary; **2.** Answers will vary; **3.** B; **4.** C